THE ULTIMATE TRANSPORTATION DEPTH EXAM

TABLE OF CONTENTS

WELCOME!!

Welcome to The Ultimate Transportation Depth Exam! Thank you so much for purchasing this book!

This exam covers 40 questions and solutions that are found on the transportation depth exam. It's built to meet the specifications based on the NCEES guidelines. It is also designed to have a similar look and feel to the real exam.

The depth exam is typically a much harder exam than the breadth. You should be spending quite a bit of your time in your depth section so that you can score well. Keep in mind though, that if you can crush the morning portion, then the afternoon will be much easier on you as they add both scores for your final score. Having said that though, you should be spending 60 to 70% of your time in your depth section.

This test is not endorsed by the NCEES organization. These are problems that my team and I have written to help you succeed in passing the PE exam. I would encourage you to take this timed to see how long it takes you. Afterwards, you can take note of the areas that you might need to work on. I have spent some time getting all of the information here for you so that it is easy to use. Each problem is labeled so you know what problem and area you are dealing with.

There are multiple ways of taking practice exams – you can work problems like homework, you can take it like the real exam - it's really up to you! I would make sure to do at least one practice exam as if it were the real deal though so you gain that experience.

As always, I value your feedback and any constructive criticism you might have on this exam or anything else we produce to help others pass. You can also get many more resources on the sites we run at www.civilengineeringacademy and www.civilpereviewcourse.com, including step by step video practice problems.

I know that with a lot of practice you will become much more proficient at working problems and doing them with less and less assistance. Keep at it and you will be prepared to pass the PE.

I don't need to tell you about the benefits of obtaining your PE license because I'm sure you already know them. You must get it to have a great career in civil engineering (and a lot of other fields!).

As always, I wish you the best of luck!

Sincerely,

Isaac Oakeson, P.E.

(You're going to have that by your name too!)

P.S. Errata for this and any other exam we've made can be found at www.civilengineeringacademy.com/errata. Also, if you're intested in jump starting your preperation head to www.civilpereviewcourse.com/freetraining for a free video series on how to prepare, take, and pass the PE exam the first time.

LEGAL INFORMATION

Civil Engineering Academy's

The Ultimate Transportation Depth Exam

Isaac Oakeson, P.E.

Rights and Liability:

In other words, please don't go copying this thing willy-nilly without giving credit where it should be given by actually purchasing a copy. Also, don't go designing real things based on these problems.

If you find errors in this book (I am human of course), or just want to comment on things, then please let me know! I can be reached through the website at www.civilengineeringacademy.com or by email at isaac@civilengineeringacademy.com.

ABOUT THE AUTHOR

Isaac Oakeson, P.E. is a registered professional civil engineer in the great state of Utah. Shortly after passing the PE exam in the Fall of 2012 he started www.civilengineeringacademy.com and www.civilpereviewcourse.com to help future students pass. He has authored and helped author various exams with his entire goal of providing the best resources for engineers to study and pass the PE.

Civil – Transportation Depth Exam Specification

I. Traffic Engineering (Capacity Analysis and Transportation Planning) (11)

A. Uninterrupted flow (e.g., level of service, capacity)

B. Street segment interrupted flow (e.g., level of service, running time, travel speed)

C. Intersection capacity (e.g., at grade, signalized, roundabout, interchange)

D. Traffic analysis (e.g., volume studies, peak hour factor, speed studies, modal split)

E. Trip generation and traffic impact studies

F. Accident analysis (e.g., conflict analysis, accident rates, collision diagrams)

G. Nonmotorized facilities (e.g., pedestrian, bicycle)

H. Traffic forecast

I. Highway safety analysis (e.g., crash modification factors, *Highway Safety Manual*)

II. Horizontal Design (4)

A. Basic curve elements (e.g., middle ordinate, length, chord, radius)

B. Sight distance considerations

C. Superelevation (e.g., rate, transitions, method, components)

D. Special horizontal curves (e.g., compound/reverse curves, curve widening, coordination with vertical geometry)

III. Vertical Design (4)

A. Vertical curve geometry

B. Stopping and passing sight distance (e.g., crest curve, sag curve)

C. Vertical clearance

IV. Intersection Geometry (4)

A. Intersection sight distance

B. Interchanges (e.g., freeway merge, entrance and exit design, horizontal design, vertical design)

C. At-grade intersection layout, including roundabouts

V. Roadside and Cross-Section Design (4)

A. Forgiving roadside concepts (e.g., clear zone, recoverable slopes, roadside obstacles)

B. Barrier design (e.g., barrier types, end treatments, crash cushions)

C. Cross-section elements (e.g., lane widths, shoulders, bike lane, sidewalks)

D. Americans with Disabilities Act (ADA) design considerations

VI. Signal Design (3)

A. Signal timing (e.g., clearance intervals, phasing, pedestrian crossing timing, railroad preemption)

B. Signal warrants

VII. Traffic Control Design (3)

A. Signs and pavement markings

B. Temporary traffic control

VIII. Geotechnical and Pavement (4)

A. Design traffic analysis (e.g., equivalent single-axle load [ESAL])

B. Sampling and testing (e.g., subgrade resilient modulus, CBR, R-Values, field tests)

C. Mechanistic design procedures (e.g., flexible and rigid pavement)

D. Pavement evaluation and maintenance measures (e.g., skid, roughness, structural capacity, rehabilitation treatments)

E. Settlement and compaction

F. Soil stabilization techniques

G. Excavation, embankment, and mass balance

IX. Drainage (2)

A. Hydrology (e.g., Rational method, hydrographs, SCS/NRCS method)

B. Culvert design, including hydraulic energy dissipation

C. Stormwater collection systems (e.g., inlet capacities, pipe flow)

D. Gutter flow

E. Open-channel flow

F. Runoff detention/retention/water quality mitigation measures

X. Alternatives Analysis (1)

A. Economic analysis (e.g., present worth, lifecycle costs)

START TEST

1. Determine the minimum Passing Sight Distance (PSD) based on the following information:

- Distance traveled during initial acceleration to point of encroachment, d_1 = 100 ft.
- Distance traveled while overtaking, d_2 = 300 ft.
- Distance of vehicle to the opposing vehicle after overtaking, d_3 = 50 ft.
- Distance traveled by opposing vehicle, d_4 = 200 ft. The opposing vehicle travels $\frac{2}{3}$ of the time the passing vehicle occupies.

a) 450 ft
b) 550 ft
c) 400 ft
d) 650 ft

2. Determine the space mean speed of 10 cars with the folowing constant speed:

Cars	**Speed (mph)**
A	35
B	40
C	38
D	35
E	32
F	40
G	40
H	36
I	40
J	30

a) 32 mph
b) 36 mph
c) 40 mph
d) 44 mph

3. A car ideally travels at a speed of 80 mph from point A to point B along a distance of 200 miles. Determine the total delay suffered by this car if the traffic encountered for the duration of the trip causes the travel speed to be reduced to 60 mph. Also, assume that the travel speed will be reduced to 40 mph for 1 mile of the trip per intersection, and the travel time will be delayed for an additional 30 seconds per intersection. Consider that there will be 10 intersections between A and B.

a) 1 hr
b) 2 hr
c) 3 hr
d) 4 hr

4. A highway with a speed limit of 80 mph has a road blockage due to a natural disaster. How far from the blockage is a signage needed to be placed so that a driver traveling at the maximum speed can safely stop? Assume that the signage can be seen by the driver when it is at most 100 ft away and the car will decelerate at 50 ft/sec^2. Use a perception-reaction time of 1 sec.

a) 145 ft
b) 155 ft
c) 165 ft
d) 175 ft

5. Which of the following choices is defined as the method for determining the quality of service on highways based from density? Hint: It varies from category A (free flowing) to F (stop-and-go).

a) Level of Service
b) Highway Density
c) Road Category
d) Level of Classification

6. A car is traveling at a speed of 90 ft/sec. The driver perceived a road blockage and applied the brakes. The car traveled along 225 ft from the time of perception to full stop. Determine the nearest skidding distance of the car if the perception-reaction time of the driver is 0.5 sec.

a) 150 ft
b) 160 ft
c) 170 ft
d) 180 ft

7. A single lane entrance to a certain highway charges a fee to entering vehicles and serves each vehicle at an average of 10 sec. Consider that starting from 8 a.m. (rush hour), an expected flow rate of 480 vehicles per hour will be decreased to 240 vehicles per hour after 30 minutes. This flow rate will then remain constant for the next hour. Since queueing is expected after 8 a.m., how much time will it take for the queue to dissipate?

a) 40 min
b) 50 min
c) 60 min
d) 70 min

8. The following table represents a certain intersection with the effective green time equal to 60 sec and the whole cycle length equal to 120 sec. Determine the capacity of the South approach.

Movement	**Approach**	**Direction**	**Saturation flow rate (pcu/hr)**
1	North	Through + Right	1800
2	South	Through + Right	1800
3	East	Through + Right	2000
4	West	Through + Right	2000

a) 850 pcu/hr
b) 1800 pcu/hr
c) 900 pcu/hr
d) 950 pcu/hr

9. A road intersection has a capacity of 4500 veh/hr. Given the following data in the table below, determine the reserve capacity of the intersection.

Days	Average 8-hour peak time Daily Traffic (veh)
Monday	35,000
Tuesday	25,000
Wednesday	28,250
Thursday	24,500
Friday	36,200
Saturday	20,850
Sunday	22,350

a) 1020 veh/hr
b) 1070 veh/hr
c) 2450 veh/hr
d) 3430 veh/hr

10. A car is approaching to a simple horizontal curve. If the internal angle of the curve is I = 35°, what will be the length of a 850 ft radius curve when the start station is STA 101+20.

a) 519.2 ft
b) 419.5 ft
c) 602.5 ft
d) None of the above

11. A vertical sag parabolic curve will be constructed and designed at a sight distance of 300 ft and a length of curve of 350 ft. Determine the required grade of descent if the grade of ascent is 1.5%.

a) -4.14%
b) -5.12%
c) -1.5%
d) -6%

12. A reversed curve of parallel radii connects and has a total length of curve of 300 ft. The length of the smaller radius is 100 ft and its internal angle is 30°. Determine the bigger radius of the reversed curve.

a) 473 ft
b) 470 ft
c) 465 ft
d) 350 ft

13. Considering a sag vertical parabolic curve of length 250 ft with an approach grade of -3.5% and exit grade of 3%, find the elevation of a station 100 ft from the start of the curve. (elevation of start of the curve = 86 ft)

a) 84 ft
b) 80 ft
c) 78 ft
d) 72 ft

14. The intersection of Sunbury Rd and Silver Rd has the following characteristics:
- Speed at Sunbury Rd = 40 mph
- Speed at Silver Rd = 30 mph
- Located in a town > 12,000 people

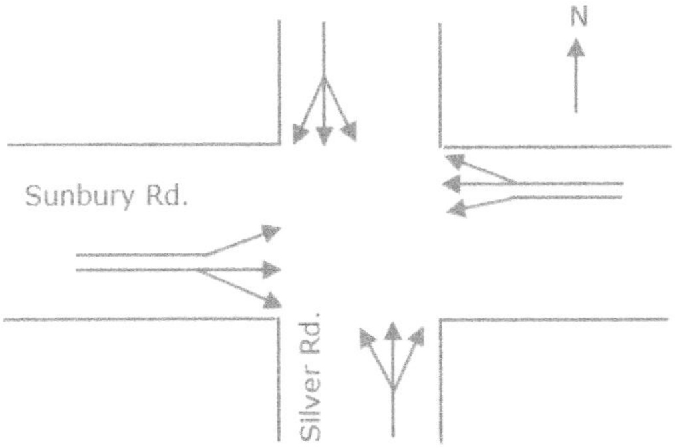

Time	Sunbury Rd - 2way (vph)	Silver Rd - North (vph)	Silver Rd - South (vph)
10.00	550	150	200
11.00	600	200	175
12.00	650	225	250
13.00	675	175	190
14.00	560	90	120
15.00	680	120	100
16.00	780	150	125
17.00	800	180	175

This intersection will be studied for a warrant analysis. Which of the following statement are true?

a) Warrant #1 is satisfied
b) Warrant #2 is satisfied
c) Warrant #3 is satisfied
d) None of the above

15. A highway curve is superelevated at 3° from horizontal. If the radius of the curve is 500 ft, find the maximum velocity that a car could run around without any lateral pressure between the tires and the pavement. Use g=32.2 ft/s^2.

a) 29 fps
b) 35 fps
c) 27 fps
d) 32 fps

16. How far from the edge of a highway can an obstruction be allowed so that all drivers can safely pass on circular horizontal curve with radius of 350 ft? The minimum stopping sight distance is 475 ft. and the total width of the road is 20 ft. Assume that the highway is single lane since it is intended for a one-way traffic only.

a) 77.5 ft
b) 48.4 ft
c) 55.5 ft
d) 67.5 ft

17. An energy cushion unit has a design speed of 45 mph with a limit of deceleration equal to 193 ft/sec^2. The vehicle has a length of 12 ft and weight of 3500 lbm. Determine whether the design is sufficient or not based from 80% efficiency.

a) Sufficient
b) Insufficent
c) Not enough information
d) None of the above

18. A car traveling at a constant speed approached a hazard on the road and smashes on the brake. If the car ~~was~~ travelled 200 ft from stepping on the brake to the total stop, calculate the approaching speed of the car. Consider that the time from stepping on the brake to full stop is 10 sec.

a) 51 mph
b) 46 mph
c) 35 mph
d) 27 mph

19. An ascending grade of +3.5% meets a descending grade of minus 1.5% in a vertical crest parabolic curve. Compute the length of the curve if the sight distance is 450 ft. Assume h_1 is 3.75 ft and h_2 is 2.0 ft.

a) 350 ft
b) 400 ft
c) 450 ft
d) 500 ft

20. Which of the following rules defines that if two vehicles arrived at a certain intersection at the same time, the vehicle on the right has the priority? Note that this rule is applied to unsignalized intersection where traffic is light.

a) Right-of-Way
b) Priority to the Right
c) Yield to the Right
d) Right Entry First

21. A curve with radius of 375 ft is banked with superelevation equal to 0.35. Find the coefficient of lateral pressure if the speed of the car is 75 ft/s. Use $g=32.2\ ft/s^2$.

a) 0.116
b) 0.114
c) 0.211
d) 0.241

22. A manufacturing company is to choose between 2 options in purchasing a heavy machine.

The first option is to avail of the delivery service costing an overall fee of $1,000. The second option is to use the company service to fetch the machine from the factory where it is to be bought.

From the company, the service will pass 2 toll gates with fees of $50 and $100 respectively. An additional fee of $50 is to be charged in each of the toll gate if a vehicle is carrying a heavy load. The necessary cost of the vehicle (i.e. gasoline) has a total of $300. The cost of hiring a driver and a helper for the whole trip is $500 in total. Determine which option is more economic.

a) Option A
b) Option B
c) Not enough information
d) Both are equally economic

23. The timing diagram of a two-phase system is shown below:

Phase 1	Green 30	Yellow 3	Red 36

Phase 2	Red 34	Green 32	Yellow 3

Determine the effective green time for Phase 2 considering a starting loss of 2 sec.

a) 30 sec
b) 31 sec
c) 32 sec
d) 33 sec

24. Given that the headway between two vehicles is 2 sec, determine the spacing of the same vehicles if they have a uniform speed of 25 ft/sec.

a) 50 ft
b) 40 ft
c) 60 ft
d) 25 ft

25. Determine the number of merging conflicts on a T-intersection illustrated in the figure below.

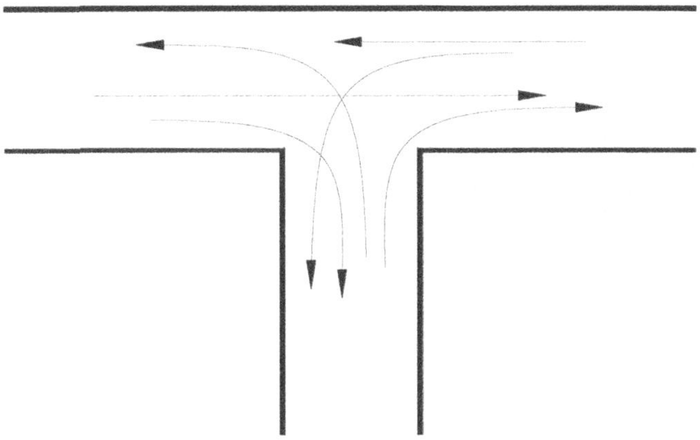

a) 3
b) 4
c) 5
d) 6

26. A 5 mile long highway is under study. It was determined that 28,000 vehicles pass this stretch of the highway everyday. For the past 5 years, the total number of accidents recorded was 6375. Determine the accident rate per 100-million-vehicle-mile (mvm) of this portion of the road.

a) 6375 accidents/100mvm
b) 2495 accidents/100mvm
c) 2805 accidents/100mvm
d) 1775 accidents/100mvm

27. Which of the following terms is defined as the total roadside area, beginning at the edge of the roadway, which allows drivers to stop safely or regain control of a vehicle that leaves the roadway?

a) Recoverable Slope
b) Embankment Area
c) Shy Distance
d) Clear Zone

28. A certain portion of a highway 3 miles in length was analyzed and the following data were recorded:

Types of Accidents	**Injury Crashes**	**Fatal Crashes**	**Property Damage**
Quantity for 2011	987	543	875

AADT = 30,000 vehicles

Determine the non-fatal accident rate per million-vehicle-mile.

a) 5668
b) 4779
c) 3458
d) 1463

29. A T-intersection was observed to collect the number of accidents per year. It is found that there are a total of 1025 accidents for the year 2010 and 2011. Shown in the figure below is the average daily traffic for the intersection. Determine the accident rate per million-entering-vehicles.

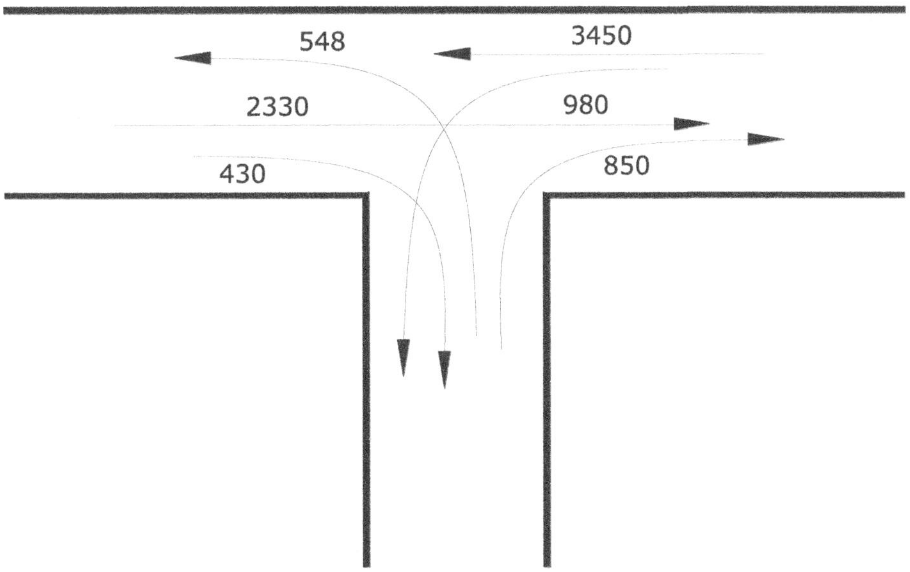

a) 164
b) 174
c) 198
d) 248

30. Which of the following terms explains the maximum safe speed when conditions are so favorable that the design features of the highway govern?

a) Running Speed
b) Design Speed
c) Highway Speed
d) Average Speed

31. Considering that a portion of a road with 9 ft wide and 500 ft length will be constructed with 0% grade. The height of fill in the starting point is 2 ft while the height of cut in the end point is 3 ft. What is the volume of the soil that needs to be filled/cut?

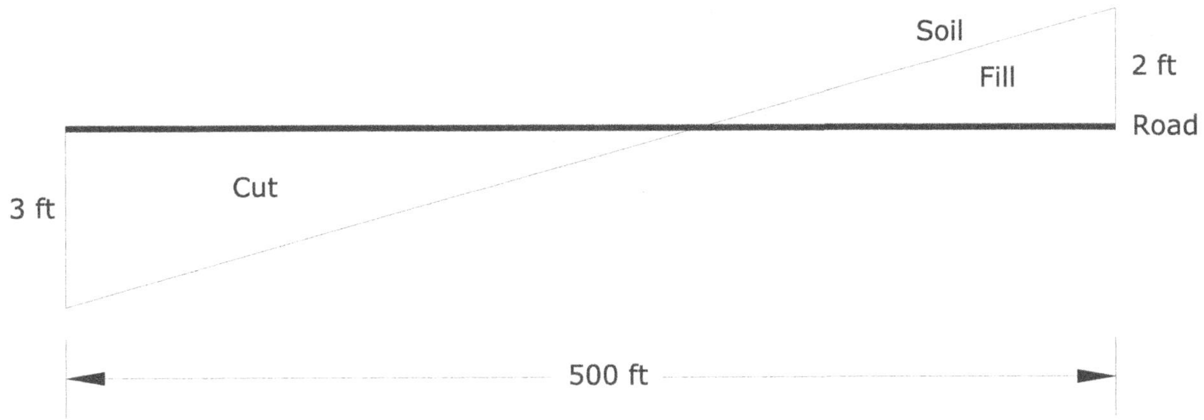

a) 2250 ft^3
b) 1250 ft^3
c) 2560 ft^3
d) 2230 ft^3

32. A trapezoidal canal with steady uniform flow has inclination angle of 45° and a base width of 3 ft with water flow of 5 ft width, find the velocity of the water flowing in the canal. Use n = 0.013 and bed slope = 0.0125

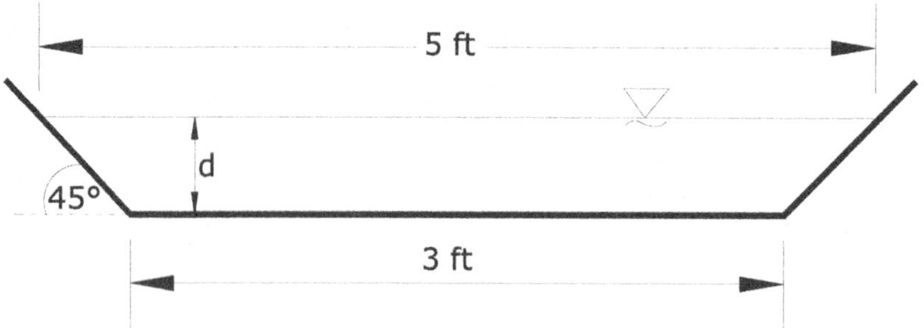

a) 7 ft/s
b) 8 ft/s
c) 9 ft/s
d) 10 ft/s

33. Water flows in a trapezoidal canal at rate of 150 cfs. The canal has base width of 4 ft and side slope of 2H : 1 V. Assuming n = 0.015 and S = 0.0015, solve for the critical depth.

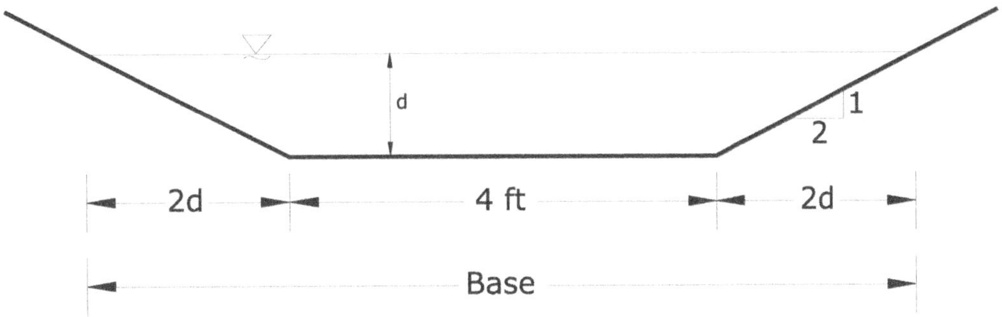

a) 2.4 ft
b) 3.4 ft
c) 1.2 ft
d) 2.9 ft

34. What is a type of hydrograph that results from 1 inch of direct runoff that is distributed uniformly across the whole watershed?

a) Direct Runoff Hydrograph
b) 1-inch Equivalent Hydrograph
c) Unit Hydrograph
d) Simple Hydrograph

35. The following data was obtained from a proctor test for a soil sample; determine the maximum acceptable limits of soil density.

Density at 5% moisture content	= 50 lb/ft^3
Density at 14% mositure content	= 120 lb/ft^3 (max density)
Density at 23% moisture content	= 75 lb/ft^3
Must meet a relative compaction	= 95%

a) 114 lb/ft^3
b) 110 lb/ft^3
c) 112 lb/ft^3
d) 120 lb/ft^3

36. A borrow pit has a soil density of 95 lb/ft^3 and moisture content of 10%. A compacted road to be constructed will need to have a dry density of 105 lb/ft^3 and a moisture content of 13%. The road will have dimensions of 500 ft length, 14 ft width and 2.5 ft thick. What is the required volume of soil from the borrow pit that needs to be hauled?

a) 22100 ft^3
b) 20900 ft^3
c) 21400 ft^3
d) 21280 ft^3

37. The following soil parameters were determined during soil investigation:

Weight of moist soil from excavation= 15 lbs
Volume of excavation = 0.105 ft^3
Weight of Water in the soil = 2.5 lbs
Percent Compaction of the soil = 95%

Solve for the maximum dry density of the soil.

a) 135 lb/ft^3
b) 125 lb/ft^3
c) 117 lb/ft^3
d) 122 lb/ft^3

38. A compacted asphalt concrete specimen contains 5% asphalt binder (specific gravity = 1.034) by weight of total mix, and aggregate with a specific gravity of 2.75. The bulk density of the specimen is 150.5 pcf. By ignoring absorption, calculate VFA.

a) 20%
b) 40%
c) 50%
d) 70%

39. What is the criterion used to determine if a certain pavement needs to be replaced, according to AASHTO?

a) Pavement cracks reach 1 inch in dimension
b) Water saturation of the pavement reaches 25%
c) The serviceability is reduced to 2
d) The Level of Service drops to F

40. The following parameters is used for the design of a flexible pavement as per AASHTO procedures.

Structural Number (SN): 3.5 @ 1,500,000 repetitions
2.6 @ 900,000 repetitions

After 900000 repetitions, an overlay will be applied to prolong the road surface life, designed for 1,500,000 repetitions in the overlay period, and the remaining capacity able to support 4,500,000 repetitions before the pavement needs to be replaced. Determine the remaining life ratio of the pavement before and after the overlay period.

a) 0.4, 0.67
b) 0.5, 0.57
c) 0.4, 0.57
d) 0.3, 0.67

PROBLEM SOLUTIONS

PROBLEM 1 SOLUTION:
PASSING SIGHT DISTANCE

The minimum PSD requirement is calculated as follows:

$$\text{Min PSD} = d_1 + d_2 + d_3 + d_4$$

$$= 100\text{ ft} + 300\text{ ft} + 50\text{ ft} + 200\text{ ft}$$

$$= 650\text{ ft}$$

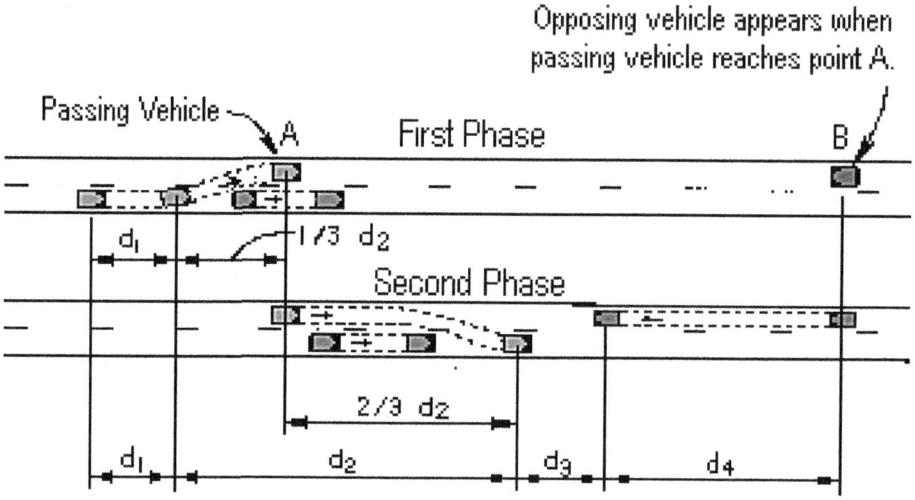

(Answer D)

PROBLEM 2 SOLUTION:
SPEED STUDIES

$$\text{Space Mean Speed} = \frac{10}{\frac{1}{35}+\frac{1}{40}+\frac{1}{38}+\frac{1}{35}+\frac{1}{32}+\frac{1}{40}+\frac{1}{36}+\frac{1}{40}+\frac{1}{30}}$$

$$= 36.26 \approx 36 \text{ mph}$$

(Answer B)

PROBLEM 3 SOLUTION:
SPEED STUDIES

The ideal time of travel = $\dfrac{200 \text{ miles}}{80 \text{ mph}} = 2.5 \text{ hr}$

The actual time of travel:

- Due to intersection, a 1 mile traffic will cause a reduction to 40 mph speed:

$$\left(\frac{1 \text{ mile}}{40 \text{ mph}}\right) \times 10 \text{ intersections} = 0.25 \text{ hr}$$

- Additional 30 seconds per intersection:

$$30 \text{ sec} \times \left(\frac{1 \text{ hr}}{3600 \text{ sec}}\right) \times 10 \text{ intersections} = 0.0833 \text{ hr}$$

- 60 mph for the rest of the travel

$$\frac{200 \text{ miles} - (1 \text{ mile} \times 10 \text{ intersections})}{60 \text{ mph}} = 3.167 \text{ hr}$$

Actual travel time = 0.25 hr + 0.083 hr + 3.167 hr = 3.5 hr

Total Delay = actual time – ideal time

= 3.5 hr – 2.5 hr

= 1 hr

(Answer A)

PROBLEM 4 SOLUTION:
SIGHT DISTANCE EVALUATION

Solve for the distance traveled from applying of brakes to full stop:

$$d = \frac{(v_{final})^2 - (v_{initial})^2}{2 \times \text{acceleration}}$$

$$= \frac{0^2 - \left(80 \text{ mile} \times 5280 \dfrac{\text{ft}}{\text{mile}} \times \dfrac{1 \text{ hr}}{3600 \text{ sec}}\right)^2}{2 \times \left(-50 \text{ ft/sec}^2\right)}$$

$$= 137.67 \text{ ft}$$

Solve for the distance traveled during the perception reaction time

$$d = v_{initial} \times PRT$$

$$= \left(80 \text{ mile} \times 5280 \frac{\text{ft}}{\text{mile}} \times \frac{1 \text{ hr}}{3600 \text{ sec}}\right) \times 1 \text{ sec}$$

$$= 117.33 \text{ ft}$$

Total Distance traveled by car after seeing the signage:

$$d_{total} = 137.67 + 117.33 = 255 \text{ ft}$$

However, the signage can be seen by the driver even it is 100 ft away. Therefore, the required distance of signage to the blockage is:

Required Distance = 255 ft – 100 ft = 155 ft

(Answer B)

PROBLEM 5 SOLUTION:
TRAFFIC VOLUME STUDIES

(Answer A)

Note:

Level of Service categorizes highway conditions from A to F. Density is the main determinant of this classification. Condition A represents the free flowing condition where vehicles are in low volume and high speed. The volume increases and the speed decreases as the level of service goes to F.

PROBLEM 6 SOLUTION:
STOPPING SIGHT DISTANCE

Distance traveled from time of perception to locking of the brakes:

$$D_1 = 90 \text{ ft/sec} \times 0.5 \text{ sec} = 45 \text{ ft}$$

Distance traveled due to skidding of the car:

$$D_2 = 225 \text{ ft} - 45 \text{ ft} = 180 \text{ ft}$$

(Answer D)

PROBLEM 7 SOLUTION:
TRAFFIC CONTROL

Arrival:

For t < 30 min : $\frac{480 \text{ veh/hr}}{60 \text{ min/hr}} \times t = 8t$

For t > 30 min : $8 \times 30 + \frac{240 \text{ veh/hr}}{60 \text{ min/hr}} \times (t-30) = 240 + 4(t-30)$

Departure:

For all t : $\frac{60 \text{ sec/min}}{10 \text{ sec/veh}} \times t = 6t$

Queue will dissipate when the arrival rate is equal to departure rate. Therefore,

$$240 + 4(t-30) = 6t$$
$$2t = 120$$
$$t = 60 \text{ min}$$

(Answer C)

PROBLEM 8 SOLUTION:
INTERSECTION ANALYSIS

$$\text{Capacity of South Approach} = \text{saturation flow rate} \times \frac{\text{effective green time}}{\text{cycle length}}$$

$$= 1800 \text{ pcu/hr} \times \frac{60 \text{ sec}}{120 \text{ sec}} = 900 \text{ pcu/hr}$$

(Answer C)

PROBLEM 9 SOLUTION:

TRAFFIC CAPACITY STUDIES

Find the average hourly traffic:

$$\text{Average} = \frac{35,000 + 25,000 + 28,250 + 24,500 + 36,200 + 20,850 + 22,350}{7 \times 8 \text{ hr}}$$

$$= 3431.25 \text{ veh/hr}$$

Reserve Capacity = Capacity – Actual hourly traffic

= 4500 veh/hr – 3431.25 veh/hr

= 1068.75 veh/hr

≈ 1070 veh/hr

(Answer B)

PROBLEM 10 SOLUTION:

HORIZONTAL CURVES

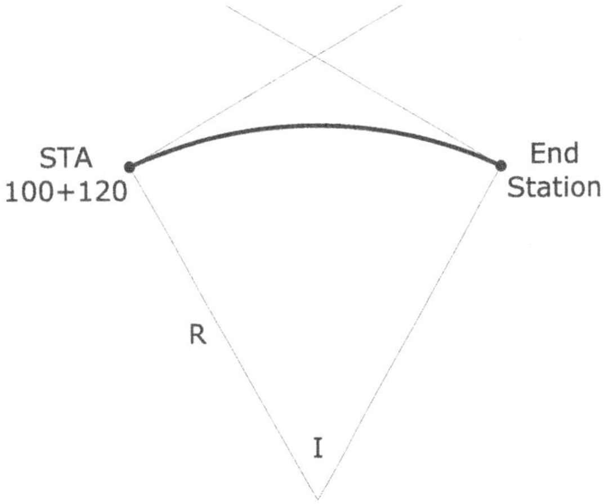

$$\frac{\pi R}{180^\circ} = \frac{L}{I}$$

$$L = \frac{\pi R I}{180^\circ}$$

$$L = \frac{\pi \times 850 \text{ ft} \times 35^\circ}{180^\circ}$$

$$L = 519.24 \text{ ft}$$

(Answer A)

PROBLEM 11 SOLUTION:

VERTICAL CURVES

Known that L = 350 ft > S = 300 ft, use this equation:

$$L = \frac{AS^2}{400 + 3.5S}$$

$$350 = \frac{\left|(1.5 - \text{grade of descent})\right|(300)^2}{400 + 3.5 \times 300}$$

$$\text{Grade of descent} = -4.14\%$$

(Answer A)

PROBLEM 12 SOLUTION:

HORIZONTAL CURVES

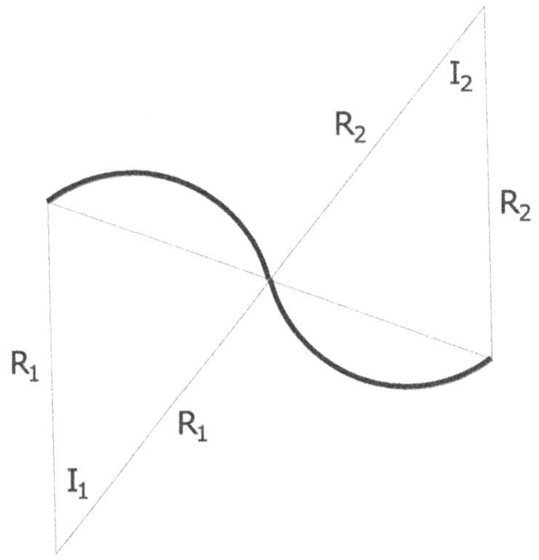

For the smaller part of curve:

$$\frac{\pi R_1}{180^\circ} = \frac{L_1}{I_1}$$

$$L_1 = \frac{\pi R I_1}{180^\circ} = \frac{\pi \times 100 \times 30^\circ}{180^\circ} = 52.36 \text{ ft}$$

Find the larger length of curve:

$$L_2 = 300 - 52.36 = 247.64 \text{ ft}$$

For a reversed curve:

$$I_1 = I_2 = 30^\circ$$

Find the larger radius:

$$\frac{\pi R_2}{180^\circ} = \frac{L_2}{I_2}$$

$$R_2 = \frac{L_2 180^\circ}{\pi I_2} = \frac{247.64 \times 180^\circ}{\pi \times 30^\circ} = 472.96 \approx 473 \text{ ft}$$

(Answer A)

PROBLEM 13 SOLUTION:

VERTICAL CURVES

Compute for the rate of change of the grade:

$$R = \frac{0.03-(-0.035)}{250} = 2.6\times10^{-4}$$

Compute for the elevation:

$$\begin{aligned}\text{Elev} &= \text{elev of start of the curve} + \frac{1}{2}Rx^2 + G_1x \\ &= 86\text{ ft} + \frac{1}{2}\times(2.6\times10^{-4})\times(100\text{ ft})^2 + (-0.035)\times(100\text{ ft}) \\ &= 83.8\text{ ft} \\ &\approx 84\text{ ft}\end{aligned}$$

(Answer A)

PROBLEM 14 SOLUTION:

SIGNAL DESIGN

From the previous information, it's clearly seen that the major street is Sunbury Rd, while the minor street is Silver Rd.

Based on the MUTCD:

Warrant #1: Eight-Hour Vehicular Volume

To satisfy Warrant #1, all volumes should meet the following values.

Table 4C-1. Warrant 1, Eight-Hour Vehicular Volume

Condition A—Minimum Vehicular Volume

Number of lanes for moving traffic on each approach		Vehicles per hour on major street (total of both approaches)				Vehicles per hour on higher-volume minor-street approach (one direction only)			
Major Street	Minor Street	100%[a]	80%[b]	70%[c]	56%[d]	100%[a]	80%[b]	70%[c]	56%[d]
1	1	500	400	350	280	150	120	105	84
2 or more	1	600	480	420	336	150	120	105	84
2 or more	2 or more	600	480	420	336	200	160	140	112
1	2 or more	500	400	350	280	200	160	140	112

Condition B—Interruption of Continuous Traffic

Number of lanes for moving traffic on each approach		Vehicles per hour on major street (total of both approaches)				Vehicles per hour on higher-volume minor-street approach (one direction only)			
Major Street	Minor Street	100%[a]	80%[b]	70%[c]	56%[d]	100%[a]	80%[b]	70%[c]	56%[d]
1	1	750	600	525	420	75	60	53	42
2 or more	1	900	720	630	504	75	60	53	42
2 or more	2 or more	900	720	630	504	100	80	70	56
1	2 or more	750	600	525	420	100	80	70	56

[a] Basic minimum hourly volume
[b] Used for combination of Conditions A and B after adequate trial of other remedial measures
[c] May be used when the major-street speed exceeds 40 mph or in an isolated community with a population of less than 10,000
[d] May be used for combination of Conditions A and B after adequate trial of other remedial measures when the major-street speed exceeds 40 mph or in an isolated community with a population of less than 10,000

Warrant #2: Four-Hour Vehicular Volume

To satisfy Warrant #2, all points should be above the curve.

Figure 4C-1. Warrant 2, Four-Hour Vehicular Volume

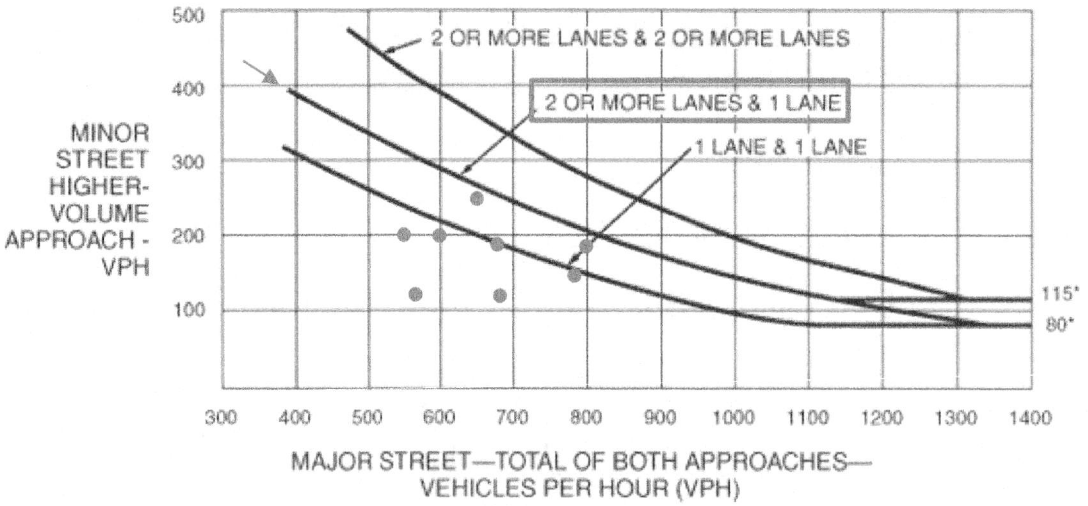

*Note: 115 vph applies as the lower threshold volume for a minor-street approach with two or more lanes and 80 vph applies as the lower threshold volume for a minor-street approach with one lane.

Warrant #3: Peak Hour Factor

To satisfy Warrant #3, all points should be above the curve.

Figure 4C-3. Warrant 3, Peak Hour

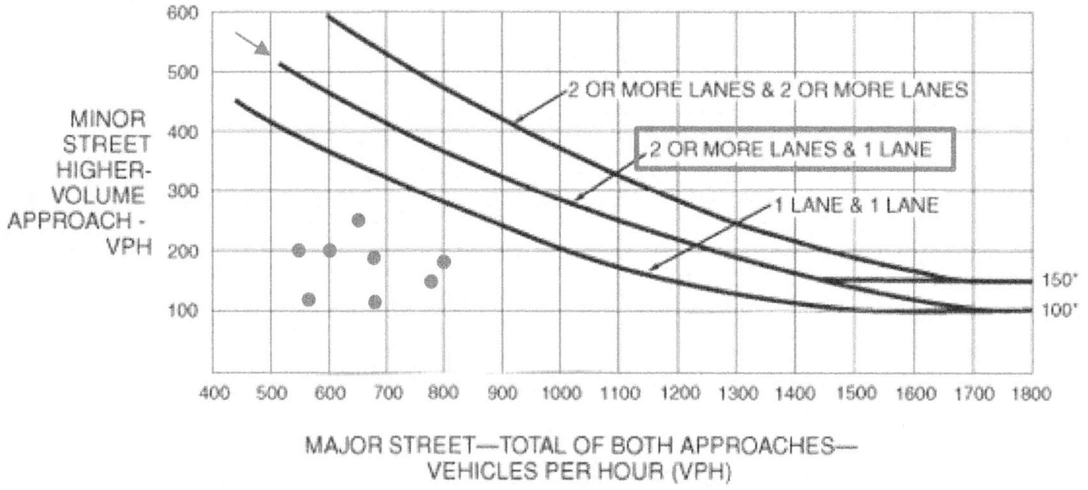

*Note: 150 vph applies as the lower threshold volume for a minor-street approach with two or more lanes and 100 vph applies as the lower threshold volume for a minor-street approach with one lane.

Time	Major Street (vph)	Minor Street 1 (vph)	Minor Street 2 (vph)	#1	#2	#3
10.00	550	150	200	-	-	-
11.00	600	200	175	OK	-	-
12.00	650	225	250	OK	-	-
13.00	675	175	190	OK	-	-
14.00	560	90	120	-	-	-
15.00	680	120	100	-	-	-
16.00	780	150	125	-	-	-
17.00	800	180	175	OK	-	-

Warrant #1, #2, #3 are not satisfied for this intersection.

(Answer D)

PROBLEM 15 SOLUTION:

SUPERELEVATION

$$e + f = \frac{v^2}{gR}$$

Compute for superelevation:

$$\tan\theta = \frac{\text{rise}}{\text{run}} = \frac{e}{1 \text{ unit width}}$$
$$\tan 3^\circ = \frac{e}{1 \text{ unit width}}$$
$$e = 0.0524$$

Since there will be no lateral pressure, $f = 0$. Solve for velocity:

$$e + f = \frac{v^2}{gR}$$
$$0.0524 + 0 = \frac{v^2}{32.2 \times 500}$$
$$v = 29.05 \text{ ft/s}$$

(Answer A)

PROBLEM 16 SOLUTION:

HORIZONTAL CLEARANCES

Solve for the internal angle:

$$\frac{\text{length of curve}}{\text{internal angle}} = \frac{2\pi R}{360^\circ}$$

$$\frac{475\text{ ft}}{\text{internal angle}} = \frac{2\pi \times 350\text{ ft}}{360^\circ}$$

$$\text{internal angle} = 77.76^\circ$$

Calculate M:

$$M = R - R\cos(\text{internal angle}/2)$$
$$M = 350 - 350\cos(77.76^\circ/2)$$
$$M = 77.535\text{ ft}$$

Distance from the edge of the road:

$$\text{Distance} = 77.535\text{ ft} - \frac{20\text{ ft}}{2} = 67.535 \approx 67.5\text{ ft}$$

(Answer D)

PROBLEM 17 SOLUTION:
ACCELERATION AND DECELERATION

Convert speed to same unit of deceleration limit:

$$45 \text{ mph} \times 5280 \text{ ft/mile} \times \frac{1 \text{ hr}}{3600 \text{ sec}} = 66 \text{ ft/sec}^2$$

Compute the deceleration and compare with the deceleration limit:

$$\text{Deceleration} = \frac{v^2}{2 \times L \times \text{efficiency}}$$

$$= \frac{66^2}{2 \times 12 \times 0.8}$$

$$= 226.875 \text{ ft/sec}^2 > 193 \text{ ft/sec}^2 \text{ (limit)}$$

Therefore, it can be considered as insufficient in length.

(Answer B)

PROBLEM 18 SOLUTION:

ACCELERATION AND DECELERATION

This is a deceleration problem.

First, solve for the deceleration in terms of the initial velocity:

$$\text{Deceleration} = \frac{v_f - v_o}{t} = \frac{0 - v_o}{10}$$

$\text{Deceleration} = \frac{v_o}{10}$ (positive since the term deceleration is already in a negative term)

Solve using equation for constant acceleration:

$$x = v_o t + \frac{1}{2}at^2$$

$$200 = v_o \times 10 + \frac{1}{2} \times \left(-\frac{v_o}{10}\right) \times 10^2$$

$$v_o = 40 \text{ ft/s}$$

$$v_o = 40 \ \frac{\text{ft}}{\text{s}} \times \frac{1 \text{ mile}}{5280 \text{ ft}} \times \frac{3600 \text{ s}}{1 \text{ hr}}$$

$$v_o = 27.3 \approx 27 \text{ mph}$$

(Answer D)

PROBLEM 19 SOLUTION:

VERTICAL CURVES

Assume that L > S:

$$L = \frac{AS^2}{200\left(\sqrt{h_1} + \sqrt{h_2}\right)^2}$$

$$= \frac{\left|\left(3.5 - (-1.5)\right)\right| \times 450^2}{200\left(\sqrt{3.75} + \sqrt{2}\right)^2}$$

$$= 450.91 \text{ ft} > S \text{ (assumption is OK)}$$

Therefore, the length of curve = 450.91 ft ≈ 450 ft.

(Answer C)

PROBLEM 20 SOLUTION:

INTERSECTION

(Answer A)

Note:

For intersection with low vexpected volume of vehicles, no control signals are being used. As two vehicles approach the intersection at approximately the same time, it is a rule of thumb to yield for the vehicle on the right with respect to the perspective of the two vehicles. This rule is called Right-of-Way.

PROBLEM 21 SOLUTION:

SUPERELEVATION

Using formula for banking of curves,

$$e + f = \frac{v^2}{gR}$$

$$0.35 + f = \frac{75^2}{32.2 \times 375}$$

$$f = 0.116$$

(Answer A)

PROBLEM 22 SOLUTION:
OPTIMIZATION

Option A: $1,000 in total

Option B:

$50 + $100	= $ 150	(toll gate fee going to factory)
$50 + $100 + $50 + $50	= $ 250	(toll gate fee going back to company)
$300	= $ 300	(necessary cost)
$500	= $ 500	(labor cost)
TOTAL	= $1,200	

Option A is more economic than option B.

(Answer A)

PROBLEM 23 SOLUTION:
CAPACITY ANALYSIS

For Phase 1:

Actual Green + Yellow = Effective Green + Starting Loss

30 sec + 3 sec = Effective Green + 2 sec

Effective Green = 31 sec

For Phase 2:

Actual Green + Yellow = Effective Green + Starting Loss

32 sec + 3 sec = Effective Green + 2 sec

Effective Green = 33 sec

(Answer D)

PROBLEM 24 SOLUTION: CAPACITY ANALYSIS

$$\begin{aligned}\text{Spacing} &= \text{speed} \times \text{headway} \\ &= 25 \text{ ft/sec} \times 2 \text{ sec} \\ &= 50 \text{ ft per vehicle}\end{aligned}$$

(Answer A)

PROBLEM 25 SOLUTION:
CONFLICT ANALYSIS

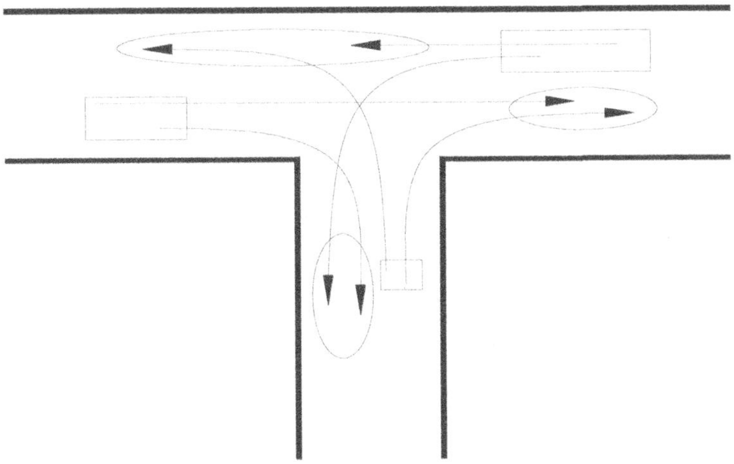

It can be seen in the diagram that there are 3 diverging (rectangular shapes) and 3 **merging** (ellipse shapes) conflicts for the T-intersection.

(Answer A)

PROBLEM 26 SOLUTION:
ACCIDENT ANALYSIS

Average Annual Daily Traffic (AADT) = 28000 vehicles

Accident Rate per Million Vehicle-Mile

$$= \frac{10^8 \times \text{no. of accidents}}{365 \times \text{time frame} \times \text{AADT} \times \text{length of road}}$$

$$= \frac{10^8 \times 6375}{365\,\frac{\text{days}}{\text{year}} \times 5\ \text{years} \times 28000\,\frac{\text{veh}}{\text{day}} \times 5\ \text{mile}}$$

$$= 2495.11 \approx 2495\ \text{accidents per 100 mvm}$$

(Answer B)

PROBLEM 27 SOLUTION:
ROADSIDE CLEARANCE ANALYSIS

(Answer D)

Note:

Clear Zone is the area for errant vehicles which may be consist of a shoulder, a recoverable slope, non-recoverable slope and a run-out area. It is measured starting from the edge of the roadway.

PROBLEM 28 SOLUTION:
ACCIDENT ANALYSIS

Average Annual Daily Traffic (AADT) = 30000 vehicles

Non Fatal Accident Rate per million-vehicle-mile

$$= \frac{10^8 \times \text{no. of non-fatal accidents}}{365 \times \text{time frame} \times \text{AADT} \times \text{length of road}}$$

$$= \frac{10^8 \times (987 + 875)}{365 \frac{\text{days}}{\text{year}} \times 1 \text{ year} \times 30000 \frac{\text{veh}}{\text{day}} \times 3 \text{ mile}}$$

$$= 5668.19 \approx 5668 \text{ accidents per 100 mvm}$$

(Answer A)

PROBLEM 29 SOLUTION:
ACCIDENT ANALYSIS

Average Annual Daily Traffic (AADT)

$$= 548 + 3450 + 2330 + 980 + 430 + 850$$
$$= 8588 \text{ vehicles}$$

Accident Rate per million-entering-vehicle

$$= \frac{10^6 \times \text{no. of accidents}}{365 \times \text{time frame} \times \text{AADT}}$$
$$= \frac{10^6 \times 1025}{365 \frac{\text{days}}{\text{year}} \times 2 \text{ years} \times 8588 \frac{\text{veh}}{\text{day}}}$$
$$= 163.5 \approx 164 \text{ accidents per mev}$$

(Answer A)

PROBLEM 30 SOLUTION:
TRAFFIC SAFETY

(Answer B)

Note:

Design Speed is used for computing the geometric design of a roadway assuming that conditions are favorable. As this speed limit serves as the basis for the design, exceeding it may promote danger and accidents.

PROBLEM 31 SOLUTION:
CONSTRUCTION OPERATIONS AND METHODS

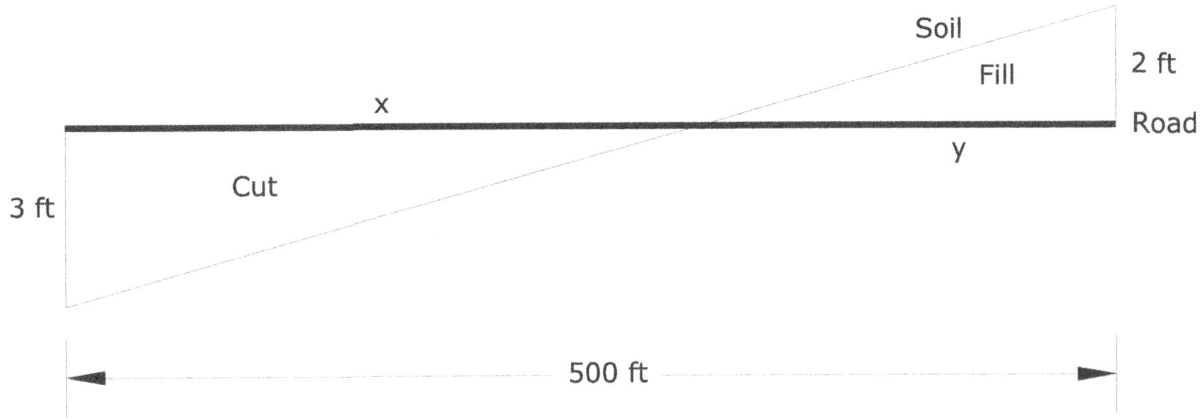

Find x and y:

$$\frac{y}{2\text{ ft}} = \frac{500\text{ ft}}{3\text{ ft} + 2\text{ ft}}$$
$$y = 200\text{ ft}$$

$$x = 500 - 200 = 300\text{ ft}$$

z is the boundary such that cut = fill. Therefore, beyond z, all will be fill.

z = 2 ft

Considering the parallelogram outside the z boundary:

$$\text{Area} = \frac{(300\text{ ft} - 200\text{ ft})(3\text{ ft} + 2\text{ ft})}{2} = 250\text{ ft}^2$$

$$\text{Volume} = \text{Area} \times \text{road width} = 250 \times 9 = 2250\text{ ft}^3\text{ fill}$$

(Answer A)

PROBLEM 32 SOLUTION:
OPEN CHANNEL FLOW

Solve for the depth d and y:

$$x = \frac{5\text{ ft} - 3\text{ ft}}{2} = 1\text{ ft}$$

$$\tan 45^\circ = \frac{d}{x}$$

$$1 = \frac{d}{1\text{ ft}}$$

$$d = 1\text{ ft}$$

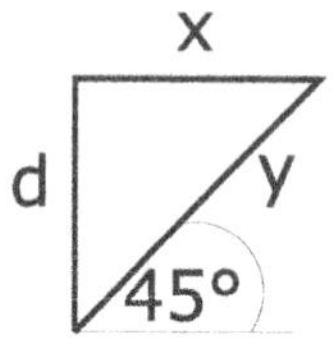

$$\sin 45^\circ = \frac{d}{y}$$

$$\frac{1}{\sqrt{2}} = \frac{1\text{ ft}}{y}$$

$$y = 1.4142\text{ ft}$$

Solve for Hydraulic Radius (R):

$$\text{Area} = (3\text{ ft} \times 1\text{ ft}) + \frac{1}{2} \times (1\text{ ft} \times 1\text{ ft}) \times 2 = 4\text{ ft}^2$$

$$\text{Perimeter} = 3\text{ ft} + 2y = 3\text{ ft} + 2 \times 1.4142\text{ ft} = 5.8284\text{ ft}$$

$$R = \frac{A}{P} = \frac{4\text{ ft}^2}{5.8284\text{ ft}} = 0.6863\text{ ft}$$

Solve for Chezy constant (C) using Manning's method:

$$C = \frac{1.49R^{1/6}}{n} = \frac{1.49 \times 0.6863^{1/6}}{0.013} = 107.645$$

Solve for the velocity:

$$V = C\sqrt{RS} = 107.645\sqrt{0.6863 \times 0.0125} = 9.97\text{ ft/s}$$

(Answer D)

PROBLEM 33 SOLUTION: OPEN CHANNEL FLOW

$Q = 150\ \text{ft}^3/\text{s}$

$P = 4 + 2d\sqrt{1+z^2} = 4 + 4.47d$

P=wetted perimeter, for a trapezoid P=b+2d(1+z²)^0.5, where z= the horizontal component of the slope, b=width of channel.

$A = 4d + \left(\frac{1}{2} \times 2d \times d\right) \times 2 = 4d + 2d^2$

Area of a trapizoid channel is = bd+zd², where b=width, d=depth, z=horizontal component of the slope.

Critical depth occurs during critical flow:

$$\frac{Q^2}{g} = \frac{A^3}{P}$$

$$\frac{150^2}{32.2} = \frac{\left(4d + 2d^2\right)^3}{4 + 4.72d}$$

Using iteration by the help of a scientific calculator or plug in the answers listed to find the correct solution:

$$d = 2.45\ \text{ft}$$

Select the closest answer:

(Answer A)

PROBLEM 34 SOLUTION:
HYDROGRAPH

(Answer C)

Note:

Every type of hydrograph can be converted into a **unit hydrograph** in which the direct runoff becomes exactly 1 inch and every flow are converted using the same factor as applied.

PROBLEM 35 SOLUTION:
SOIL PROPERTIES

Optimum moisture content is the mositure content at the maximum density:

The maximum density occurs when the mositure content is 14%.

$$\text{Acceptable limits of density} = \text{Maximum Density} \times 95\%$$
$$= 120\ \text{lb/ft}^3 \times 95\%$$
$$= 114\ \text{lb/ft}^3$$

(Answer A)

PROBLEM 36 SOLUTION:
SOIL COMPACTION

$$\text{Volume of the compacted soil} = \text{length} \times \text{width} \times \text{height}$$
$$= 500 \times 14 \times 2.5$$
$$= 17500 \text{ ft}^3$$

Note: Mass of solids (M_s) will remain constant despite the compaction process.

$$\gamma_{dry} = \frac{M_s}{V}$$
$$105 \text{ pcf} = \frac{M_s}{17500 \text{ ft}^3}$$
$$M_s = 1837500 \text{ lbs}$$

(also equal to the M_s of the soil in the borrow pit)

Use the moisture content (w) of the soil in the borrow pit to find mass of water (M_w):

$$w = \frac{M_w}{M_s}$$
$$0.1 = \frac{M_w}{1837500 \text{ lbs}}$$
$$M_w = 183750 \text{ lbs}$$

Therefore, the total mass of the soil in the borrow pit is $M_s + M_w$:

$$M_{total} = 1837500 + 183750 = 2021250 \text{ lbs}$$

Utilizing the wet density of the soil in the borrow pit, the volume of the soil needed to be hauled can be solved:

$$\gamma_{wet} = \frac{M_{total}}{V}$$

$$95 \text{ pcf} = \frac{2021250 \text{ lbs}}{V}$$

$$V = 21276.32 \approx 21280 \text{ ft}^3$$

(Answer D)

PROBLEM 37 SOLUTION:
SOIL PROPERTIES

Solve for the dry density:

$$\gamma_{dry} = \frac{W_s}{V} = \frac{W - W_w}{V} = \frac{15 - 2.5}{0.105} = 119.0476 \text{ lb/ft}^3$$

$$\begin{aligned} \text{Maximum dry density} &= \frac{\text{dry density}}{\text{percent compaction}} \\ &= \frac{119.0476}{0.95} \\ &= 125.313 \approx 125 \text{ lb/ft}^3 \end{aligned}$$

(Answer B)

PROBLEM 38 SOLUTION:
PAVEMENT DESIGN

Assume total volume = 1 ft^3

Determine mass of mix and components:

Total mass $= 1 \times 150.5 = 150.5$ lb

Mass of asphalt binder $= 0.05 \times 150.5 = 7.525$ lb

Mass of aggregate $= 0.95 \times 150.5 = 142.975$ lb

Determine volume of components:

$$V_b = \frac{7.525}{1.034 \times 62.4} = 0.117 \text{ ft}^3$$

Because of no absorption, $V_{be} = V_b = 0.117$ ft^3

$$V_s = \frac{142.975}{2.75 \times 62.4} = 0.833 \text{ ft}^3$$

$$V_v = V_m - V_b - V_s = 1 - 0.117 - 0.833 = 0.05 \text{ ft}^3$$

$$VFA = \frac{V_{be}}{V_{be} + V_v} \times 100\% = \frac{0.117}{0.117 + 0.05} \times 100\% = 70\%$$

(Answer D)

PROBLEM 39 SOLUTION:
PAVEMENT DESIGN

(Answer C)

Note:

From the AASHTO procedure for the design of pavement structures, it was required that if a serviceability of the pavement was reduced to 2 from a scale of 0 to 5, that certain pavement needs to be replaced.

PROBLEM 40 SOLUTION:
PAVEMENT DESIGN

Before the overlay period:

$$\text{Remaining Life Ratio} = 1 - \frac{900,000}{1,500,000} = 1 - 0.6 = 0.4$$

After the overlay period:

$$\text{Remaining Life Ratio} = 1 - \frac{1,500,000}{4,500,000} = 1 - 0.33 = 0.67$$

(Answer A)

SCORE SHEET

Correct Answers: ___________

Percentage: (correct answers)/40 = ____/40 = ______

Some things to note:

If you can absolutely crush the morning exam then the depth section will be much easier on yourself. You should still shoot for a high score here, but just know if you can get in the upper 90% in the morning then you just need to score more than 20 correct in the afternoon. Imagine if you got all 40 correct in the morning – you'd only need to get 16 right on your depth exam (56/80=70%)! A total of 70% is *about* the passing score for the PE. What's interesting though, is that the depth section will dominate your study time. So, put in the time and practice and you will get there. Keep at it!

LAST SECOND ADVICE AND TIPS

I wanted to wrap up this exam with some tips that I found helpful when I took the exam. Hopefully, they will help you:

1) Make sure you fully understand what your state board and the NCEES requires of you to take the PE exam and to receive your PE. Comply with all rules.
2) You typically need about 3-4 months to really study for the PE. Map out a schedule and study your depth section first. This will allow you to make any adjustments as you get closer to test time. I personally broke down the specification into the 5 major categories of: water resources, transportation, geotechnical, structural, and construction, and spent a couple weeks on each topic with more time devoted to my depth section.
3) Practice everything with the calculator you are going to use on the real exam. You need to become intimately familiar with it.
4) Know where your exam is, where to park, and where you will get food (if you don't plan on bringing your own). Don't be stuck trying to figure this out on test day. You'll regret it.
5) Review courses help. If you can't get motivated, or need the extra help and accountability they offer, then consider taking one. It's worth it to get your PE and get that boost to your career. If you're wondering which one, refer to our helpful tools below.

Helpful Tools:

We have built www.civilengineeringacademy.com to help any civil engineer become a PE. We have tons of free video practice problems there to get you going. We also have plenty of tips, must have resources, advice on courses, and more practice exams that cover your depth section. In addition to this, we have created a civil PE review course that can guide you step-by-step through the entire exam. You can check that out at www.civilpereviewcourse.com.

Made in the USA
Middletown, DE
12 September 2020

19163056R00053